In these keening poems, Daniela Naomi Molnar seeks solace in glaciers, and the ice responds. A stern but patient tutor, ice illuminates a cerulean path through grief. It is a lens for seeing ourselves in proper perspective, a prism that reveals the full spectrum of human experience. Glaciers remind us that "the only promise / time makes / is to be ongoing".

Marcia Bjornerud, professor of geosciences (Lawrence University), author of *Turning to Stone: Discovering the Subtle Wisdom of Rocks*

In the Jewish tradition, the kaddish, the mourning prayer, is simultaneously a song of praise for the unutterable, for that which is beyond all language, all praise. Here too Daniela Naomi Molnar has written a kaddish for our moment, for a glacier lost to melting, for ancestors known and unknown, that is simultaneously an exaltation for all that changes and in changing lives on: "let the pre-name turn to name / then let the name turn nameless." With incredible precision of syllable and sound, of rhythm and movement, these poems of astounding beauty beseech us to attend to the earth's own memory, which is our own memory, for as these poems know, we are not other than the earth with which we live. "I apprentice myself to the immaterial." Amen.

Julie Carr, author of *The Garden*

Is a glacier a memory? Is it time? An echo of the past? In Daniela Naomi Molnar's *Memory of a Larger Mind*, the glacier is an incantation, a kaddish, something both primordial and fixed, a thing so sentient it is at our mercy. Molnar brings us to the ice and embodies the lyric with a vision and clarity that comes only from grief. She asks us, "When a memory goes / what flows into its gap?" Here, Molnar is thinking as much about inheritance as the nature left behind, the ways that time and its bodies are at once an "insouciant menace" and a shared gossamer thing. There is a feeling in Molnar's poetry of a ruptured deity captured in the calving of ice, hope transmitted through witness, and a millennia-deep ache for that which has

always already moved through ice and stone. *Memory of a Larger Mind* is an astonishing collection of poems, one of the best books I've read in years. It will take your breath away in its insistences and urgencies.
Natalie Eilbert, author of *Overland*

Like a glacier, Daniela Naomi Molnar's poems carve and clarify their readers. This book of poems asks us to slow with its hefty task — to untame the distance between remembering and forgetting, to feral our future ghosts. Daniela excavates indifference with muscular language, investigative silence, and undiluted sentience, offering us opportunities to remember the global body with our own. Unshrinking from the onslaught of erosion, erasure, and amnesia, each poem annunciates what endures after we, and the world, are broken. Daniela shows us that all grief cuts towards a bedrock of love.
Nina Elder, artist

also by Daniela Naomi Molnar

CHORUS, Omnidawn Publishing, 2022

PROTOCOLS: An Erasure, Ayin Press, 2025

MEMORY OF A LARGER MIND

Cover art by Daniela Naomi Molnar
Cover design by Rebecca Leffell Koren
Cover typeface: Suisse Intl

Interior design by Daniela Naomi Molnar and Laura Joakimson
Interior typeface: Garamond and Suisse Intl

Library of Congress Cataloging-in-Publication Data

Names: Molnar, Daniela Naomi, 1979- author
Title: Memory of a larger mind / Daniela Naomi Molnar.
Other titles: Memory of a larger mind (Compilation)
Description: Oakland, California : Omnidawn Publishing, 2026. | Summary: "Written in collaboration with glaciers, these luminous poems are elegies and love songs, celebrations and laments. They are plein air poems, written outdoors and illuminated by shifts of light, wind, sound, and scent. As our world moves from ice to water, these poems move, too: cycling from grief to love to joy and back again, along the way asking how to withstand and transform."-- Provided by publisher.

Identifiers: LCCN 2026020231 (print) | LCCN 2026020232 (ebook) | ISBN 9781632432285 trade paperback | ISBN 9781632432346 epub
Subjects: LCGFT: Poetry
Classification: LCC PS3613.O474 M46 2026 (print) | LCC PS3613.O474 (ebook)
LC record available at https://lccn.loc.gov/2026020231
LC ebook record available at https://lccn.loc.gov/2026020232

Published by Omnidawn Publishing, Oakland, California
www.omnidawn.com
10 9 8 7 6 5 4 3 2 1
ISBN: 978-1-63243-228-5

MEMORY OF A LARGER MIND

DANIELA NAOMI MOLNAR

OMNIDAWN PUBLISHING
OAKLAND, CALIFORNIA
2026

POEM FILMS:

WWW.DANIELAMOLNAR.COM/WORK/MEMORY-OF-A-LARGER-MIND/#POEM-FILMS

North to night, a timeless reach. North to trace the vacancies of self, family, culture, earth, ice. North, seeking a mirror in a fractured expanse.

So far north, Polaris stands directly overhead: I am north with nowhere northward to go. The waning moon circles me. My compass points north, then south, then north again.

Daylight in the October Arctic is wan and brief. But what light it is — jewel-toned, thick with hue but thin, dry, and crystalline on the skin.

The light echoes and shatters, refuses to be still. Undoing all it touches, it reveals the immaterial within the material. Ice, water, time, self — in this light, all dissolve to distillates. This light demands surrender.

To grieve is to learn to remember and forget.

The Arctic light teaches me this unsteady two-step. I see the world as it's changing: memories melting, turning to water, to light. The disorientation feels like home.

I'd thought I was searching for orientation and resolution. But, here, lodged in the liminal, flooded with light — this is rest, the center I'd been seeking. It feels like a place, *the* place, where I can both remember and forget.

In the eye of a hurricane, the air is calm. Birds enter at the tip of the spiral and let themselves be drawn inward to the center, where they glide long distances, carried by the storm. Some die of exhaustion, trapped in the eye by the surrounding winds. Others surrender and survive, drawing energy from the chaos, riding the storm without becoming it.

The body is a lens to look through with the mind. In going north, I relied upon the water of my body, heavy with grief, to pull me to the eye of forgetting and remembering, the still point of that spin.

There, I stopped searching for stability and allowed myself to be moved. I found that we and the world are broken like a seed split open, fastened to the planet's mantle and ready to start anew.

In my classroom years ago, I asked my students about their favorite place in the world. One said her favorite place was inside an airplane, watching a prolonged sunset. This student was an orphan. She'd spent her life in the foster care system, being transferred from one home to another. She had aged out alone. I stared, caught fast. Can a point in constant motion be a home?

The air is calm. I press my hand to the glacier's winnowing blue, feel its primordial mind press back. I apprentice myself to the immaterial. I touch my grandmother's hand, I hold my cat's paw, I feel the hum of his purr today though it's been years since he died, and years before that when she taught me to sew, and so many years before that when the ice found its form, which was years before she died and years before I will die.

We are in motion. We are motion. Always and now.

1

MEMORY OF A LARGER MIND

Kennicott Glacier / Ahtna Nenn' and Dënéndeh, July

"What the memory repudiates controls the human being. What one does not remember dictates who one loves or fails to love."

JAMES BALDWIN

"I remember having this feeling growing up that I was haunted by something — that I was living within a family filled with ghosts. There was this place they knew about; I had never been there. Yet I had a memory for it."

REA TAJIRI

1

When a memory goes
what flows into its gap

When a glacier goes
what flows into its gap

What is memory's counter-substance
What is memory's twin

What liquifies its solid
What ethers its stuff

What tolls its hollow
What recoils its strike

We breathe shared memory
also known as air

We drink shared memory
also known as river

We are made of shared memory
Nothing is not made

of shared memory
Yet each body's memory

is gossamer, wobbly
a newborn insect

mostly iridescent wing
lurching on a leaf spine

in memory's strong wind

2

Sitting with a glacier
in the far north
of North America
in 2023
I have a memory
of being
on my grandmother's balcony
in Cluj, Romania
in 1936 when she was twenty-three
Yet I wasn't there

Sitting with a glacier
in the far north
of North America
in 2023
I have no memory
of being
with this glacier
when I was twenty-three
Yet I was here

Earlier this summer
I stood in a street
in Cluj, Romania, in 2023
staring at my grandmother's apartment
where she had lived when she was twenty-three before being
rammed into Auschwitz.
I remember resting
her/my hand
on the curve
of the black iron balcony
a cup of gold tea
soft chamomile steam
bustling square below

Now I stand by the glacial river
its swift magnificence
its insouciant menace

I was twenty-three when a truck
inside of which I sat
rammed into this barricade
above this glacial river
backed up then
rammed into this barricade
again twice thrice
rammed into this barricade
and my head
I am told
hit the windshield glass
once
twice
thrice
above this glacial river

the glass
I am told
smashed

I lost

the means

to make a memory

Why did I survive
Why did she survive

Why did she survive
from her iron-rimmed balcony
to a steel-barbed field of barracks
concrete slots terrible holes
walls — bodies — barricades
a drowning air they shared

Why does she survive
in this body, mine

This body in time
is a rumor
of an echo
of a shadow
of a fog

Upriver the glacier
drops orange and green rocks
from far and long ago

along its melting edge
it gives a memory
of aerial crags

and thin bright wind
to the valley
who didn't live it

3

A glacier is a predator of inarticulate space,

shifting space to pattern.

I wake on the glacier before dawn, walk and laugh

by the absent moon in deep blue. Footfall, footfall.

I slake my thirst with rocks, iron sharp and living.

I cup a palmful of river to see

the river's silt is magnetite and light : a brain's same twinning.

I kindle a fire on the krummholz.

Look at all those faces in the knife where it's seen flame

so naked and slow. We drift from no center to no end.

4

A glacier is a ghosted god : restless and feral.

A glacier shimmies and bulges, eats whole trees.

A glacier is a hungry lip

shouting lost language as it recedes.

A glacier is a ghost of future ruin.

Inside the glacier

water wakes

and seeps, a zero.

You / I are ghosts

among ghosts

inside ghosted gods.

Which is what it's like, now, being alive.

Pray we fail the final ghosting.

Pray the spectacle melts.

5

glacial cave striations short on-ramps to the infinite —

where long blue memories melt

to whatever

memory

becomes

unremembered

glacial cave striations ancient gates listing open

inside each gash

a cantering collapse

and a canter

can go on

and on

and on

glacial cave striations   sharp snares of now

gouges of dense gravity

asymmetries of origin

not stasis, equilibrium

the membrane moves always

even through ice and stone —

6

Scree

strewn on the glacier's mottled toe

wide fluid thinking in those stones

wide phenomena tucked

into stripes, craters, slicks, rounds

in schist, cobalt, gold, black

in lavender and granite

in dense quartz light

in moose tooth and turquoise

in slivers of copper and steel

visual heft

palpable heft

scree

soothes, anchors

my restless thinking body

capering over moraine —

upbraided sinew

across bone and socket

smooth as clouds

swaddling mountain claws with cotton, bringing rain

7

Glacier : swath of scar
pale incandescent aqua

Glacier : web of dream veins
ancient ocean iced

Glacier : tablature, terrain
rift — ridge — dip
bands of black, celadon, silver, gray

Glacier was and glacier left
and took whatever
glacier meant to move

Glacier : body of riverine logics
spinal and vertebral
domed like a skull
rucked like a rib
concave like hunger
or the entree to a hole
or concave like a palm
cupped to hold

Glacier : grizzled skin
pocked and fissured

Glacier : water mind
alluvial flesh
glacier memory melting
rivulets and rivers
striations and folds
old skin breaking
fractal and scarred

Glacier : a memory
a prediction
no origin
spreads like light

8

Glacier holds
light long
bends it blue
light long
enough to offer
the story of its journey
to reach me here
light blue
like sunset light in hue
but stranger texture and heft
light long
slides slow
smooths my skull top
then down my scapula
as the thick
gray glacial river
licks its banks clean
a predator relishing its kill

something like memory
memory beyond identity
memory of a larger mind —
immanent in the phenomena
memory inside melting
time radiant aqua blue
drips cold metronomic
tastes briny
very clean

What does the glacier know?
What memories are dying?

The scientist says thirty years ago
this swamp was glacial river
Now I see drowning alder and willow
I see gasping stomata —

We walk farther
The scientist says thirty years ago
this still gray lake was glacier
Thirty years of melt is less than my lifetime
It's thick and dark as a milkshake
A silt-clogged melt-lake the size of a city
Visible from space

The scientist then
drifts into memory
the kind he holds inside
his private ice
he says slowly
two sex workers
saved him when his wife
lost her memory to a tumor
(he says prostitutes)

We cannot own or hold
each other
we cannot own or hold
each other very long
safe from harm

The scientist resurfaces
The scientist says
the children swim here
pointing at a scintillant aqua pond
cupped in sharp black scree

The scientist says see
we've moved time
we're walking at the bottom
and the top of time
the glaciers carved the mountains down
peeled these lower layers for our feet

2

TRAP

"Death is a knot undone."

EDMOND JABÈS

"What goes too long unchanged destroys itself.
The forest is forever because it dies and dies
and so lives."

URSULA K. LE GUIN

Who forgot symbiosis
Who forgot predator/prey
Who manufactured predator
Who codified prey
Who forgot how to love the thing
before killing it

Who forgot death's fecundity
Who forgot the osmotic anthem of love
Who forgot the smell of soil breathing
Who forgot dawn
Who forged dawn unconvincingly —
sallow electric rot

Who convinced dawn of nothing
Who found dawn recalcitrant,
habitual, leaking light
Who knew nothing about survival

Who couldn't forget melanin
Who couldn't forget money
Who imagined well the distance
between soil and cerebellum
Who kept that distance tame,
leg in a trap, screaming —

Whose leg was in a trap
Whose trap was made of plastic
Who felt it and felt it and felt it
sever and tear

Who finally died there
Whose body was eaten by ravens
Whose fur lined nuthatch nests
Eyes eaten, too
Sockets cupping mushrooms
in the spring

3

YOU / I

"All water has a perfect memory
and is forever trying to get back to where it was."

TONI MORRISON

"I require a You to become; becoming I,
I say You. All actual life is encounter."

MARTIN BUBER

1

Water is *pliant attentiveness.*

Matter *which resembles nothingness.*

Water comes from space. *Most, if not all water on this planet came from countless small comets thumping against the atmosphere.* Our bodies, our lives are inextricable from space — a realm that exceeds our comprehension. Without this mystery, we die.

Water's molecular shape is crystalline: throw water at the ground and it lands locked together but freely hinged so it molds, as one, to everything it touches. No other form of matter holds and molds this way.

Water's surface tension allows it to be a body: drop body, river body, sea body. Some water bodies have their own linguistic homes: riverbed, sea floor. When one water body touches another, they bond instantly — smooth surgery, memorized. All other matter, broken, stays broken. Each water body is a portion of water's fused and *continual flow of awareness.*

All water is related. Water is relation. Water does not, cannot, forget its relations. *I am surprised that when a hair dryer falls into a bathtub we are not all electrocuted.*

2

Ice is water's awareness, slowed and sculpted by eons of earth.

Ice is a poised vector in geologic time.

Ice retains water's pliant attention
water's flawless memory
water's nothingness
water's vast grasp.

We can walk on ice.

We can slow with it.

3

two coyotes call the dawn
fog frozen air to song

as molten copper light
pools across ice

ice time gapes time
coyote call : response

dark discs of dead
cottonwood leaves

and a long sine sun
morphs the zeroes

of the pond's ice eyes
i try to unmap

make space in the self
for the coyotes' trill and yelp

their whorled songs
dig dig carve

dense strata down
to the solace of indifference

to my own persistence

4

You / I : each have two bodies
a familiar fleshly form
and a global body
shared and cast
throughout the biosphere

You / I : feel both bodies daily
when we drink water, breathe air
we touch our global body
this is not abstract

You / I : spill, are simultaneous
in all space and time

You / I : the spaces-between, the time-between
the spaces-of, the time-of

You / I : are each an archival commons
in ongoing flux
warped by sense and memory
which exceed the subjective :
Stars are holes in the dark
when I look at one, I go there

So as the world is hurt
suffers empties cries
a firm refusal to cleave or dull
is a type of tenderness, a way to stay

You / I : are sensory commons
    made of negative bodies
    electrons' first name
    Nothing is not
    made of negative bodies
    including space
    and negative bodies
    are mostly made
    of negative space
    blank, conductive, alive
        to negative capability
        the power of not-knowing
        and not needing to know,
        unlatching lyric possibility —

when I look at one, I go there

You / I : a pine tree in Auschwitz
    and an Oregon elm
    a dead tulip and a rocket
    a plastic bottle cap / a bone

You / I : inexorable porosity
    borders break and break again

You / I : aggregate habitats
    More microbial than human cells
    form a human body

You / I : glacial melt in Athabasca
    rising tides in Guam

You / I : buy a mango from Ecuador
    in a store made of Canadian fir
    purchased with a piece of plastic

    made of fossilized animals
    who breathed and died
    billions of years ago
    in a hot, distant swamp

        You / I : hear the air
            its dearth of birds
            its excess of engines
                You / I : combust
                You / I : uncanny
                You / I : ordinary sense depth
                        global presence, uncontained

5

A dream moves through
the dying cat, twitching his paws.

Some life force is voided
so he can be dreamed.

The imagination is meant for what the mind cannot endure.
Seasons are slowly

drifting out of place. Time and space
disunifying as in a dream. *One day the distant*

glacier will come ripping through the tissue of my body —
through the tissue of every body —

With mounting desperation we are drilled
on the importance of borders —

You / I must be boundaried. Be either here or there.
Don't be all

over the place.
Don't spill the limits of your skin —

one day the distant glacier —
You / I have to be all

over the place
because you / I already are.

The glacier, too, is being dreamed.
No paws to twitch, no whiskers.

But have you seen it? The glacier's veins
coursing with that searing, seeing blue?

The glacier, too, is being dreamed on its way to dying —
being dreamed by what, by who?

By me, by you.

4

A NAME IS ITS OWN PLACE

For J.L.F. and S.F.

"The seam that fuses doubt/faith, optimism/ despair [...] – that seam holds for me a kind of light, and a capaciousness. A way of living that seems to clarify. The holding of opposing forces makes me feel like a catfish, looking off in both directions at once. It also keeps curiosity alive."

LIA PURPURA

"Time is the one thing
we can all agree to call supernatural."

HALLDÓR LAXNESS

Kaddish 1

if this world is dreamed
if it is rhyme, a scheme
a calling across and through
the name inside the name

then even if i cannot
always love the world
i can love the dreamer
for this rhyming dream

i can love the dreamer
who dreams the day
to rhyme with its own light
who dreams the vanished
to rhyme with my life
who dreams the zero
to rhyme with the one

i can love the dreamer
by redreaming a dream awry
i let the icicle's why
turn to whylessness
inside a thirsty mouth

waking at the very end
of this world's dream
i can thank the dreamer
for the tree roots and rootlets
talking poems eating bones

for all the waters
their shared subjectivity
a big dream i can drink
a big dream i must drink
in order to live

for the sap
of the blind bee's honey
sapsame i can gather
the pollen of the last wild field
and offer it to my hive
hoping one of us remembers
the way to make matter sweet
or make a word
sweet enough to hold
its own origin and echo
like oh like ah
like the deathless air

let us let
air unhinge and widen
allow the rhyme of the dream to breathe —

Kaddish 2

Let the dream carve
a tunnel in your trachea
for breath then name
Let the name be lush
Let the name be rangy

roaming past time

to the source
of language :
a clean huddle
of ash —

the only promise

time makes

is to be ongoing

an inconclusive light that cannot dim
forming
pink organs and petals
green fuses and rot
the metastasis, the ribosome, the cilia, the cell,
the twelve dollar cup of coffee
the animal with ground-down teeth on the tundra
the quake the rubble the flood
the traps sprung on sinew

in inconclusive light

god a fermata

descend the broken air

note the air's new tunnels
paved with snapped beaks
and the silence of the new heat

Kaddish 3

slacken the hallow
billow the place
skull the bloom
ocean the life
slacken the name
river the vein
slacken the billow
fluent the node
puddle or harbor or sound

slacken the place
swell the hallow
song the source
braid the billow
slacken the name
unknot the skull
node the pith
bloom the soil
stone or mountain or spit

slacken the other
slacken the us
slacken the i
slacken the task
slacken the air
slacken the name
billow the name
node the place
lung or storm or vent

maybe the seed
maybe the flesh
maybe the mud
maybe the firth

maybe the mouth
maybe the moon
maybe the us
maybe the gold
maybe the ash

slacken the word
skull the space
billow the spool
blood the wide
hum the one

Kaddish 4

the whole surface grammar eating sun : face the faceless one

have you seen nothing : see you

everywhere everything everyone : eyes of the faceless one

asphalt puddle eye : hi : can you feel

held by being seen : can the seeing calm your sight

can you let the seeing pry

can you be its prey : looking looking back

hi a stone's compass eye : hi the predator who hides inside the sun

the faceless gathered all the waters : fire flocked to every hollow

made sight

Kaddish 5

time come
time come
time come

the central shine in matter
not dead yet
succulent ventricles

plush with blood
shove the non sequiturs of our forms
into a slippage of camellia in cold winter sun

distend the dialectic to a thicker sound

allot the eye its magnet sight

chant the day its compass name

life the stone its ever home

mind the muscle of air its I

breathe the I its naming

I the time its changing

Kaddish 6

My grandmother's fist smashes glass
six decades on, my mom's voice
shatters and blots —

does anything subside
can we lie

down with this
implosion, coax it finally to sleep

can we lullaby a wrecked amen
embellish unrest with rest —

Magnolia tilting open
can you unclench the fuchsia
of her palm
open it like a throat

set to sing. Survival
is the dark's start

above the falcon's field
which has suddenly gone noiseless as her shadow coasts

across her prey
making a memory in the prey that will stay —

and feel real
even when the falcon's gone —

a vivid and reasonable
hallucination —

Kaddish 9

below the quick] [surface currents of your mind

muscular water moves] [undiluted sentience

in a sole and fluid flow] [through everyone

your tongue can disown the dead] [multiplication

and disregard the sad arithmetic] [of the bad plan

you don't need to call the failure] [any name. calve instead an inoculant

omission] [of the self

to make a home of hinge] [let that zero

loll] [open

be muttered or sung] [muttered or sung

by the nameless one] [a sound thick

as no] [mirror

Kaddish 11

dear elk spine
i char you black
i pulverize you to color, name you paint

dear glacier rock
i palm you
i pulverize you to color, name you red

dear trees pulverized to paper
with water as ligament,
i name you substrate, name you skin

together we make an uncontained brain
of ruptured water, cracked earth
divided fire, split air, whole electric

we write our name on water
we are faulty nervine locks
not for but of

Kaddish 13

take three steps back
bow the head to the left
straight ahead
right
straight ahead
down

take three steps back
do not look up
do not feel the sun on your skin
do not feel

take three steps back and stay there
as three steps in front of you
the living shimmers
stay there
let it turn to salt

take three steps back
recall the broken as a dazzle
not a lack
take three steps back
note the blind spot in being
what did you expect? an overview?

take three steps back
the poet who killed himself is lucid
the one who lives perplexes
death too creates order
an open eye can help

the world neither hides nor reveals
as it winnows itself toward dream
the sensory devolving
and with it the ways you've learned to live

take three steps back
try to feel under nothing
an open eye can help

Kaddish 14

All winter the sky was a bandage through which light scarcely seeped

from the puncture wound of sun. Now spring pulls

pink and green from gray. A thinking surface looks

just like an unthinking one.

Sockets appear in my paintings as if they wish to move.

Stand up if you mourn. Let weight strengthen bone.

That's how a name is made. A name must endure

all the ways to its emptiness. A name contaminates and sweetens

by blurring solitudes. A deer sits stranded, watching nameless traffic move.

Her gaze renames the street. A bare seep. The world is an act

of will. It will be complete. But not yet.

Kaddish 15

may this world be finished soon say

inside a day quickly say

finished inside your body say

quickly as long as the world say

may the name be made say

assent cry dilation say

gleam loft frill say

gild air refrain say

may the name be stubborn say

may a silence blanket quickness say

may the asymmetry stay

Kaddish 16

bees sip lavender flowers
wind transposes trees

yesterday has nothing
to do with today

today has nothing
to do with tomorrow

both wrong grief and right grief
dwell within each day

only one expects to stay
tomorrow as today

wrong grief has loaded
my dreams with bullets of clocks

has melted the scarlet
moon to minor wound

has made a right-angled circuit
of a lungful sphere

has bit the crusted marrow
from the dry bone of reason

has broken each of my teeth
and filled them with feeling

unbearable to air

air to unbearable — the dream

wakes me to tell me
about my feet. that they are still here.

start with your feet
says the dream's right grief.

you'd been gone two days
when the dream woke me
and led my feet to a crow

in a tree above an alley
in pre-dawn rain
walk this alley said the crow

he spoke to me
from his branch above my head
he cawed and cawed at me

leaning his gleaming
black beak at me saying see see
saying here here here

i looked i tried
to see i could not see
in the pre-dawn gray rain

lost, i began
to walk back up the alley
no said the crow

no you have not seen
swooping nearly touching
my head he lassoed me

back here here here
see see

i walked back up the alley
look again said the crow

look

again

three times the crow and i
danced with sight this way
he looped air to tug me back

when i walked away
three times until i saw
you

just below the crow
a tiny tuft of wet fur
i lifted you
in my fingers
to my face
your scent

and i saw
what the crow
had seen

the story he was sharing
of where and how
you'd gone

he knew me, knew you
or he was me, was you
is me, is you —

he showed me
your tail next
tucked below

chain-link steel
he gave me your story
he gave me your broken

skull, a few clean teeth
gifts saying

look again look again see see see

then he led my feet
to your foot
your leg had been gnawed to the bone

your soft paw remained
you'd been
so close to home

you'd been going
the way of decay

i'd loved your decay
your withering, a gift

i had thought
we had more days together

you found your own way

look again said the crow
see see see

Kaddish 17

the polished green stone, horizon-breadth, the color
of your eyes

glows up
from your circular grave look again

lilac scabiosa and still clear water
in its gray stone trough look again

fireweed poised to bloom, bright magenta petals clasped
by tight green bracts, waiting for a cue

lupine, violets, goldenrod, tufts of sun
and ear-soft sage the color of your eyes look again

wrong grief makes
a fearful god of fear

a viscid haze
in which all sight gets stuck

right grief is a neighbor bringing you a cup
she's made of clay

it's a pocked, imperfect body like all bodies made
of various opacities and vast invisibles look again

Kaddish 18

too much freedom
creates not nothing but nothing's raised scruff

wrong grief is too much freedom

we do need our forms

our feet, our paws, our ice, rocks, moraines,
beds, mountains, currents, homes

we need them   then
we need to let them go

let the pre-name turn to name
then let the name turn nameless

wrong grief grips the name
            slicks it with sweat and tears, the liquids of the living

                        death is dry

                                let the name dry   to light

                                        its tuned math
                                        its hinged doors

                                        its atomic emptiness
                                        its done black stars

                                        let its dryness spark holes
                                        in the wet of you

wrong grief endures
right grief evaporates

and unfolds the inner
rhymes and creased chords
compressed by the I of living

right grief looks again
an open orb of eye

wrong grief
constricts in the light

dilate, says the nameless

look again

                    look again

                                        see see see

5

MATTER IS METAPHOR

On a sailboat in the Arctic, October

"What remains of the self
Unwinds into a vanishing light, and thins like
    dust, and heads
to a place where knowing and nothing pass into
    each other, and through"

MARK STRAND

"in the air, there your root remains, there,
in the air"

PAUL CELAN

1 4 October, Tempelfjorden

this archipelago once lived
at the planet's bottom as a tropical swamp
it drifted ineluctably up
to the planet's top
impelled by restless flow

then it froze and was folded
into dentate peaks by time

gypsum, limestone, granite, and shale
ice-flecked and pressed with tropical fern and fin

long ago this rock rose from the warm sea
and the animals clambered to learn
land's magmatic demands
how to live the rucked and monochrome
rock rock rock —

where foxes script elegies with their paws in the snow
where red rocks shout, imploded by cold
where lenticular clouds croon as they script the dark gullies
where the dwindling
archive ice refracts a half-lopped moon

glossing the glacier with a lustrous storm
in stunted flux, an anesthetic glare

as the glacier's calving gashes wide the air —

the glacier is soon to be a symbol
before becoming
nothing again —

we all learn to curl around a central absence
becoming what we can't recover from
what we can't conceal

2 5 - 6 October, Billefjorden

I wake from dense dreams
snarled in a net of ifs.

Long dawn snow
glows terracotta / teal, backed by black sea,

each form moored by cobalt shadows
bent across the soft white earth.

One reindeer skull bristles in a fringe
where skull succumbs to antler,

each strand at that juncture
limned in shadow-stalks of blue —

the dead dream too
steady and slow

in pumpkin-colored lichen and fine mats of lavender heath
in tundra pocked by whopping rocks

who hurled themselves to write
lines of their passage

like the striated tides
also scribed on the pebbled plain.

Incandescent aqua of the glacier's bared teeth —
yes grimace yes smile —

and the morning's half moon
swoops slow and wide,

lassoing polaris at the top of the sky.

3 7 October, Fuglefjorden, Svitjodbreen, and Holmiabukta

pink light empetals ice
slow and precise
on ragged cursive cliffs
above a plucked green sea
asking again
how to see

slept berth-rocked
slowed
at the planet's apex
where molecules barely move
where heft, form, exigence
circulates and drifts
to nonspecific pivots asking again

how to see
past the cove of expectations
into the crenelated ice, into the memory…

little I, insipid eye, how to see
oneiric ice
when it traps ideation
its intelligence
a net of slow primacy, slow injury

the humans' arms sweep
a story of the shore, wild
arcs of explication

airlessness of glacial blue
a planar ovation
billowed by informant cold

lavender light now

freezing as dreaming
to death
yes what else

4 8 October, Fuglesongen and Ytre Norskøya

press skin / to the ice's ponderous glow : pink, black, palest blue,
lavender, lime, mauve
colors quicken

in the light, soft-sharp and stable-changing : edgeless
contradiction here / at the edge of things
the thinness is thick as tar
and consummate as air
we breathe it in

a sharp crescent in the dome
and my compass gone inverted
so close to the pole but

peach light on sheer white is all i need of alignment,
an invitation to the waning
decrescendo decrescendo decrescendo —
while the hull cuts brash ice
and light sidles sheer over remnants of land,
against conclusivity and we
too are fermata,
time signature undefined ((((((

5 9 - 10 October, Nordaustlandet, Murchisonfjorden, and Kinnvika

Glacier exists in how it instantiates love. Your bare palm pressed against the glacier. The rest of your body, still.

Glacier exists like a last animal exists, non-breeding in a zoo.

Glacier exists in the swerved tern's long migration. She casts her hollowed-out name in a big penumbral blur across the glacier's nowhere light.

Glacier's cleaved tongue must touch-talk with the ocean or its black veins swell, its blue goes gray. Thunder is pummeled each time a glacier dies. Pulsed into the tides.

Glacier is the radiance its stubborn body casts. Its cyan sluice of light. It exists in the traces left after things detach.

The glacier becomes an algorithm, a hound sicked on its own scent.

Floating, melting orphan ice. Existent drift.

Glacier flings boulders to careen over plains, scribing dented elegies, long palimpsests that gather into cursive wails.

Glacier's memory exists unbound to any form of matter.

We press our skin against a glacier's skin to see if we exist.

We press our skin against a glacier's skin to make a neural route, alter atoms in the commons.

Glacier is its own absence, stalks its own void.
Makes more   room there.

Glacier's dying breaths will kill us. This is symbiosis.

Glacier furrows into hungry gaps, gulping humans and foxes and polar bear cubs. Glacier is cackling and wants us to cackle, too. The cackle reshuffles the adjacent possible as possibilities retract. As glacier's bared teeth bite back.

On the floe, a black wing
    torn from its torso, sinew bright
against the blue, feathers spread.

    It's one thing to daily ransom
an abstraction of ice
    and another to touch its dwindling skin.

The axis
    tips, currents totter,
standardization intensifies

    the virtual demand.
The world's rim is thick
    with black fireworks

of calving, the clang
    of collapse
towards which the birds fly —

    as improbable loops
of late human minds
    seek a selvage of solutions

and ice turns to water
    and water turns
sensate and specular, a muscular conduit

    of memory
torn by this teal hull
    which blasts a path

through the ice's ancient mind —
    The ebbing
current spills into the sound, lost

    where the black soles of islands
are licked clean of aqua ice.
    What is more elemental:

water rock air ice
    or the fire that's shifting
it all to memory?

6 11 October, Spitsbergen: Gimlebreen and Bockfjorden

One sunrise cloud on the ice horizon, a lit helix listing north
to the pole, magnetic, inaccessible
where time clicks then blurs —

the eyelid's prayer weight

rests on nothing,
on zero, proportioned to

each lunar blue,
and the earth's blood below

coursing cadmium now
— subflux, the dreaming,
the cartilage of light
cloaking the nude bone snow.

The horror's widening wake.
The shore's black stone, licked clean of any alibi
or story of survival, a valuable fat
squandered long ago —

7 12 - 13 October, Bockfjorden, Jotunkjeldene, Liefdefjorden, Hornbækpollen

— swift excision from the cyclic
by the deeply cleaved and addled
late human mind

eons of matter's metaphor, dissolved for profit's thin directive

— even god's listing eye
would clone itself
to see this mess
with any depth —
any clue to this inscrutable, murderous
vexation of the self — the cyclic
cannot hold, it's skidding open now
here's a gash in the integument — goodbye, love, goodbye —

here's a glitch in the processional
rippling error out —

a shattering finality —

the moon whets
and arcs its gaunt spine
against the night's pale numerics,
says, we're long past the crash —

whatever grief i've brought here
has been made microscopic by the vast, frozen
ache of this place
its beauty is its closure, terminal as the sun

the sun contorts the sky —
an I is a bare
decision of distance
or fear and fear again

I strain to see that remnant cache of ifs
as the cliff glowers in collapse —

8 14 - 17 October, Krossfjorden, Fjortende Julibukta, Kongsfjorden, Hornbækbukta, Dahlbreen

— fricative song of glacial skin, fading fast into the

human
mind that perceives
human
mind that is a part

the rickety seam between —

blue rock
is shattered into angles
by extremities of cold

and blue light climbs
arpeggios of air
skirting stars and opening the ocean —

we move fast to the decrescendo, resounding through decline —

the late unbroken is this light

this light, a whole ethics

matter's sustenance
and catalyst
and memory
dissolving
far past human spans

6

CALVINGS FOR THE SENSIBLE

For C.B.

"Typically what cannot be seen
Is what we most like to see.
Longing is my favorite
Material for engaging (not picturing,
Not illustrating) holes.

So when I say
Holes are conduits or 'a means to'
Or space, or intersection –
I mean holes are occasions –
Opportunities which can take
Many forms materials and durations
(Imagine a hole that has only duration)."

POPE.L

"The times are urgent; let us slow down."

BÁYÒ AKÓMOLÁFÉ

emergency patience

the emergency is patient

I sense slow

a new dense sensorial tense

yielding the unbearable, obliquely borne, a scaffolding
for the past's impasse with the future perfect

or how the lifeline, broken, stays its tack

or how to track the light's distortion to know what fracture is —

I want the calving
to hurl back the impropriety

none of the above —
human operator —
No.
unclick the leash

I want to make my life
a rejoinder to the long-dead query,
to find my unfurled eye and furl my I

then unratchet the binary, swim the resultant flood

love gulf, a swelling, swallow saltwater hard

I'll drift just askance of the miasmic, find water's perfect memory, still free

I'll find intelligence is a flat refusal to be unporous skin
reduce my immunity to suffering
listen to archaic organ wisdom from within

I'll storm inconsistencies guarded by common sense
pierce the common epistemic, hear its deflating whine, find its
syncopated rhyme

grease Nothing's machine

watch change, be changed, unfinal and unclear

note the heft beyond   the event horizon

sound out a new chord with the extinct

        be way off key and listen

it's a deep economic guffaw

or a prayer short of god

it's a chalk outline of the atmosphere

which says inside — it's time

to unwhiten my knuckles — I think the glacier wants to play

wants to blot out acquiescence with its endogenous light

wants me to say the shape of the sacrifice zone

and to thank the mirrored beetles set to feed —

wants me to detonate the grim banal,
mine the pragmatic to its terrified core and blast it, silently

wants me to dive
into the cold paralysis
and the hot paralysis
to go numb, liquify, and see what I dream
let sweat and melt refract my open eyes —

the glacier wants me to not fail at love

to refuse to abide by each color-coded slot

to learn to spurn both the bleak and all notions of salvific

and to see what follows, what follows, and then what follows that —

7

NEW BLURS

"Naturally, the immaterial alone is new."

ÉTIENNE SOURIAU

the glacier says there's an ocean i must touch

as the distinction gives way

to the brindled ice flashing past color into light

and memory sagging open to a steady zero

we curl around, becoming

wider, wiser unrecovered

uncovered unconcealed

i slept dreamt by the berth

and woke asking what if i refuse, ever again,
a straight line

what if i commit to the symbolic purposive beyond teleology

what if i choose to love the tilting subsong more

than the swell of song

what if i try to torque the line of my brief time, twist its conductive
bundle towards this new light

to feel the honest dissonance i must touch

when a memory goes what flows into its gap
when a glacier goes what flows
into its gap   the offing, the far oceanic where
i'm told by light   that light
is memory's counter-substance, light is memory's twin —

water's pliant attention   forms and remembers   all life
light alters the otherwise   insular cycles of life

the glacier's memory   is hinged to light
                    is waxing   to light, light exceeding

human grasp of space and time   so we strain to see it
                    look again   look again   see see see

we call it   a glow   as black
kittiwakes flash
white underwings across
new blues, new blurs, new light made
of the sky's superannuated cache —
the new light wants

circumscription by a body
so it can alter memory — future, present, past

it will drift from form to form, waiting patient eons
for a lung, a ligament, a moraine,
for a stone or a river, an organ or a vein
for a hungry, spacious node to enter and to change —

NOTES

0

A line from Ama Codjoe's poem "On Seeing and Being Seen" is referenced: "My body is a lens / I can look through with my mind." This poem appears in Codjoe, Ama. *Bluest Nude* (Minneapolis: Milkweed Editions, 2022).

YOU / I, SECTION 1

"pliant attentiveness. The matter which resembles nothingness."
Weil, Simone. *First and Last Notebooks*. Trans., Richard Rees. (New York: Oxford University Press, 1970), 111.

All other italicized words in this section are from: Childs, Craig. *The Secret Knowledge of Water* (New York: Back Bay, 2000), 89-90.

YOU / I, SECTION 4

"Stars are holes in the dark / when I look at one, I go there"
Berssenbrugge, Mei-mei. *A Treatise on Stars* (New York: New Directions, 2020), 5.

YOU / I, SECTION 5

"One day the distant glacier // will come ripping through the tissue of my body — / through the tissue of every body —"
These lines are inspired by:
Hildyard, Daisy. *The Second Body* (London: Fitzcarraldo Editions, 2017).

Several phrases in this book first appeared in my book *CHORUS*.

ACKNOWLEDGEMENTS

Thank you to the editors of *Attached to the Living World: A New Ecopoetry Anthology*, published by Trinity University Press, s, for publishing a previous version of Part 1, No. 4.

Thank you to Julian Stettler for including a previous version of Parts 1 and 2 in *The Glacier is a Being*, published by Sturm & Drang Verlag (Zurich, Switzerland), 2023.

Thank you to Chamber Music Northwest, for featuring "Kaddish 1" and "Kaddish 3" in concerts and programming during the summer of 2023.

Thank you to *Blood Orange Review* for publishing previous versions of "Kaddish 2" and "Kaddish 9."

Thank you to *Laurel Review* for publishing "Kaddish 1," "Kaddish 2," and "Kaddish 3" in *Breaking the Glass: A Contemporary Jewish Poetry Anthology* in Fall 2023, Issue 56.1.

Thank you to Emmi and everyone at *Buckman Journal* for publishing excerpts from Part 1 alongside related paintings from my New Earth series in Summer 2023.

Thank you to *Poetry Northwest f*or publishing excerpts from Part 1 in Summer 2024.

Thank you to Ayin Press for publishing excerpts from Parts 1 and 3 in *Otiyot* in 2024 alongside some of my photographs from the Arctic.

Thank you to The Arctic Circle residency, The Wrangell Mountains Center, and PLAYA. This book would not exist without your support. Thank you for the gift of time, space, and place.

O

Cultures that live closely with glaciers know them to be sentient. Sit with a glacier, listen to water's deep whistle through its rills or the roar of a collapsing edge. Sit with a glacier and you will hear and feel and see a living being in the throes of death.

In this book, I've tried to articulate what I heard the dying glaciers say. In doing so, I recognize that I've inserted myself into a long, ongoing conversation between the lands, the waters, and their indigenous communities. I'm an outsider and a newcomer. I love the far north but these places are not mine; they are the traditional, ancestral, unceded lands and waters of the Ahtna Nenn' and Dënéndeh peoples (Kennicott, Alaska) and the other-than-humans who inhabited Svalbard and its surrounding waters before European colonization. (Svalbard is unique in that there is no record of humans living there until European explorers laid claim to it in the mid-16th century.)

I've prioritized listening rather than speaking in every exchange. I recognize that my work is a vanishingly small part of a much longer and deeper story. My goal is to honor that story by helping to shift the broader culture of which I am a part.

O

Thank you to Jason Francisco, Tobi Kassim, Casey Boyle, Michael Johnson, Rebecca Clarren, Emmi Greer, and Liz Lampman (*z"l*) for reading and offering vital insights on drafts of this work.

Thank you to Anne-Sophie Balzer, whose PhD thesis focuses on Parts 1 and 2 of this manuscript. Thank you for the honor of your close readings, and for all the ways you enact your belief that poetry can make and remake the world.

Thank you, Ara, for the cup.

Love and thanks to Anne Germanacos, Linda Puffer, Nina Elder, and the congregants and cats of Poetry Church. Your friendship and care sustained this work more than you might know.

O

Love and thanks to Mom, Dad, and my entire family. And to Rosalie for the directives, and for letting me go.

Michael, thank you for seeing, naming, inspiring, loving, and putting up with the nimbus. I love you. Always and now.

O

To grieve is a courageous and vital act, especially at a time when there are so many incentives to do otherwise. To grieve is to love, to love is to grieve. This book is a *makom* for all who allow themselves to do so.

Daniela skipping rope in the Arctic Photo by Elizabeth Philotera Bourne

Daniela Naomi Molnar is a poet and artist who creates with color, water, language, and place. Her art centers on memory — planetary, cultural, familial, and personal. She works with pigments she makes from plants, bones, stones, and specific waters such as rainwater and glacial melt. Poems and essays are created alongside the visual art; the practices overlap and influence each other. Her debut book *CHORUS* (Omnidawn) won the 2024 Oregon Book Award for Poetry, followed by *PROTOCOLS: An Erasure* (Ayin Press), a finalist for the National Jewish Book Award. Her work leads her to far-flung places but she loves orbiting back to her studio where the forest meets the city in Portland, Oregon. danielamolnar.com

Memory of a Larger Mind
by Daniela Naomi Molnar
Cover art by Daniela Naomi Molnar
Cover design by Rebecca Leffell Koren
Cover typeface: Suisse Intl

Interior design by Daniela Naomi Molnar and Laura Joakimson
Interior typeface: Garamond Premiere Pro and Suisse Intl

Printed in the United States by Books International,
Dulles, Virginia on Acid Free Archival Quality Recycled Paper

Publication of this book was made possible in part by gifts from
Katherine & John Gravendyk in honor of Hillary Gravendyk,
Francesca Bell, Mary Mackey, and The New Place Fund

Omnidawn Publishing

Oakland, California